Learning About Reptiles

Jan Sovak

W0006902

DOVER PUBLICATIONS, INC.
Mineola, New York

Bibliographical Note

Learning About Reptiles is a new work, first published
by Dover Publications, Inc., in 2001.

International Standard Book Number
ISBN-13: 978-0-486-41851-3
ISBN-10: 0-486-41851-0

Manufactured in the United States by Courier Corporation
41851004
www.doverpublications.com

Introduction

Unlike mammals (including humans) and birds, which are warm-blooded, reptiles are cold-blooded—their body temperature changes according to the temperature of their surroundings. These creatures are not suited to cold weather and are found in warm locations. In this little book you will read about lizards, snakes, turtles and tortoises, and alligators and crocodiles. As you learn about the 12 reptiles, you will be able to place a colorful sticker on each page of the book.

Green Anole

The Green Anole's habitat ranges from Virginia to Texas and as far south as the Florida Keys. This member of the iguana family grows to between 5 and 8 inches and lives in trees, vines, and tall grasses. The male's throat expands when it is excited. This lizard turns green at night but is brown during the day. It eats spiders, beetles, moths, and flies.

Galápagos Tortoise

These giant animals live on the Galápagos Islands, off the coast of Ecuador in South America (*galápago* means turtle in Spanish). Few have survived into the 21st century. Ships' crews used them as food in the past, leading to their near extinction. Their shells range from dark gray to black. These creatures may weigh over 400 pounds. Their diet consists of fruits and plants.

Chameleon

The chameleon is known for its ability to change color, which it does in response to light or temperature. It may also change color to signal its mood to other creatures. Chameleons are found in the Mediterranean region, North Africa, sub-Saharan Africa, and India. The smaller chameleons eat insects, and the larger go after small birds and lizards.

Regal Horned Lizard

This creature grows to between 3 and 6 inches in length. Its head is covered with large spines that form a "crown." It lives in rocky and sandy areas of the American Southwest and Mexico. The regal horned lizard is active during the day, especially the early morning. Its diet consists of insects, which it catches using its thick tongue.

Northern Black Racer

One of several racer snakes, this fast-moving creature's habitat extends from Maine to the Carolinas, Georgia, Alabama, and Mississippi. It lives in fields, woodlands, meadows, and the grassy banks of streams. Its favorite foods are large insects, lizards, frogs, small rodents, and birds. This snake buzzes like a rattlesnake when it is disturbed.

Western Painted Turtle

From 4 to 10 inches in length, this turtle has a smooth olive or black shell and yellow and red stripes. It is found near the Canadian–U.S. border ranging from Ontario and Missouri to Oregon and British Columbia. A young turtle will eat whatever meat is available but becomes plant-eating when older. Its habitat is shallow rivers and streams.

Gila Monster

One of two venomous (poisonous) lizards, the Gila (**hee**-la) monster is found in Utah, California, Arizona, New Mexico, and Mexico. This thick-bodied reptile may reach two feet in length and weigh over three pounds. It eats small birds and rodents and other lizards. It stores fat in its tail to live off of when food is scarce.

Crocodile

The fearsome crocodile lives in marshes, swamps, and rivers in Florida, Africa, Asia, and Australia. Its adult length varies from over 20 feet to barely 4 feet. As a result of being hunted, however, the larger crocodiles have become rare. Young crocodiles eat small animals, insects, frogs, and crabs, moving on to fish, mammals, and birds as they mature.

Leaf-toed Gecko

This creature has toe pads with tiny suction cups, which permit it to travel up walls and across ceilings! Geckos make the most noise of any lizard, and the leaf-toed variety makes a squeaking sound when it is startled. It comes out at night and feeds on insects and spiders. Its habitat is rocky areas of the desert in southern California.

Loggerhead Turtle

This member of the sea turtle family can be found in both the Atlantic and Pacific oceans. It has paddlelike limbs and a heart-shaped shell. At one time loggerheads weighing more than 1,000 pounds were observed, but the development of their habitat for use by humans has reduced their numbers. They eat many types of sea creatures, including sponges, mollusks, and sea urchins.

Alligator

Alligators are the largest North American reptiles. Their habitat varies from rivers and lakes to bayous (creeks or marshy bodies of water). When in the water, this reptile may show only its eyes and nostrils. The use of its skin for clothing items and the destruction of its habitat have reduced its numbers. It eats birds, fish, turtles, and small mammals.

Glass Lizard

This legless creature looks like a snake but is really a lizard (it has eyelids and ear openings, which snakes do not have). It can be found in grasslands and woodlands throughout North America. Like other lizards, this creature sheds its tail when alarmed, but the tail comes apart in several pieces, like shattered glass. It eats insects, small mammals, and other lizards.